Butter on Toast

Poetry: Volume II

S. E. McCarty

In loving memory of
Phoebe McCarty

Bite Your Tongue

All dressed up to celebrate with friends,
With hugs and smiles we take our seats to dine.
We share our stories, listening, sipping wine,
Sparks of interest, careful none offends.
Round the table, subject changes hands,
Dancing near the elephant in the room.
Knowing looks, cautious words assume
Not everyone can take what truth demands.
The waves nearby don't hesitate to roar,
A drunken neighbor says what's on his mind,
And well-placed jokes are with candor lined,
But we resist the craving to say more.
      Keep to breezy tones and shallow chatter.
      Bite your tongue. Does it really matter?

Free Will

In the playroom

      Spread a game of no-rules Risk

      Or sketch a smudged drawing with rainbow chalk,

      Start a chess match with a subbed-in knight

      Or get on the PS4 to battle plants and not-dead zombies.

In the playroom

      Fifteen or so throw pillows are apparently thrown

      To lie in corners, under the table, in all positions

      To challenge Pokemon cards and baseball cards

      With Legos-of-no-instructions.

Anything goes

In the playroom.

You are Safe and Free and Allowed

In the playroom.

Butter on Toast

Sleep, shut your eyes my love
and sleep.
Find your energy again and
forget your long day of work
and worry and effort.
Count, up, to, 100 and
then down again
til your lids are soft blankets on
your bright and youthful eyes.

Sleep, and shut
your world away, my love,
until a fresh sun arrives and
gives you new hopes and second tries.
Close the curtain to your
mind's performance and dance
again tomorrow, for tomorrow
another show will play for you,
another game,
another adventure.
You will need your strength
and all the color of dreams
to settle a ripe dispute or
meet the next challenge.

So sleep, my love, and rest
your hands
so they are ready to help your
buddy beside you,
and your feet
so they are fast to find the

right path for you and others,
and your little brow
covered with matted mess,
so you can have the courage to
smile at someone
when that's all they need in this lonely world.

Rest up, and sleep sound,
not just for your sake but for
all the rest of us
weary-eyed strivers who are
drowned in misery and dried
of all relief.
Sleep, my love, and inhale
some peace of mind
so when we meet again in the morning
you can spread it like
butter on toast.

You Remind Me of My Son

Right this way, if you please, kind sir.
His Majesty will see you now.
Listen close as he tells you how
Productive your deeds really were
        Now all is said and done.

"Your parents taught you about me,
And you have loved me ever since.
Others followed to penitence.
The love you shared is your best deed.
        You remind me of my son.

You sought to know me as the cure
In a church hymn or in my book.
Blessed are they with eyes to look
For beauty as my signature,
        The world my inspiration.

You took your place as last in line.
You gave until you'd given all,
And that is the gist of my call.
Blessed are the poor ones, for thine
        Is the kingdom of my son.

The way you treated all you met
With kindness and humility
Produced fruit in great quantity,
Multiplying fish in the net –
        That reminds me of my son.

Yes, do come in, believing child,
You have done well as a steward,
And now I will give your reward,"
He welcomed me in as he smiled.
   "Look who's finally here, Son!"

Slipping Away

She sleeps more and eats less
Slower, quieter, eyelids confess
There's a source of hidden pain
Pulling back like a ball and chain,
The once vibrant river of motion
Now a dripping motivation.
  And Time will make the call
  With shrill whistle and black flag
  To declare that he wins after all,
  Bored of stagnant drag.
    All I can do is hold her drooping gaze
    And hand, caress the resting head
    That lullabied my sleepy soul to bed
    And loved me into life so many days.

Buckshot

One leg over, and no amount of warning will make her turn back
        from the ledge she has determined will make her burdens
lighter   She has been cut down by her estranged father's
death, her job's rigidity, and of course the threat of Covid on her
high-risk child.   Now she licks her wounds, believing
that this final leap might bring her back to herself   Back
to her vibrant youth when kids were fun and motherhood was
exciting and marriage wasn't a tension in her day.   The
wounds have spread like buckshot and every compartment bleeds
the life drop by drop, every day the dripping more   terminal,
        so that now she has just the energy left to tell me
that, sigh   it just didn't work out with him and she is
ready to be on her own, by herself, to lick her wounds in a lonely
corner of a new house she'll share with, sometimes,   just the
cat.   How to tell her that she is making a mistake.
Maybe she isn't.   How to assure her that things can get
better, now that the kids are back in school, her job is easier, and
Covid is getting under control   She has time to pull her one
leg back, to give it all more time, to try something new, to save
herself   and her family; but she smiles at me   with a
light in her eyes and her dirty martini raised to reassure me that
she'll be   fine.

Death 'n' Taxes

"Nothing's sure 'cept Death 'n' Taxes."
Nothing's set, friends say to me,
"But don't let's talk 'bout politics!
"It's impolite." I disagree.
Let them speak.

    I could tell ya scores of stories,
    Oh, you wouldn b'lieve my tales.
    Folks so scared, they feel me comin',
    They reach their knees. They weep and wail,
    To no avail.

    I ain't plannin' to quit my bizness,
    Ain't my call, just my job.
    Y'all can lock down all ya want,
    But that don't mean ole' Death will stop,
    'Cuz I will not.

    You make me out to be the bad guy –
    Some from age, some of illness.
    Man can kill more than a plague:
    In war, abortion, and violence.
    Own your sins!

    But 'nuff 'bout me, I'm gettin' preachy.
    My good ole' buddy, Tax, is here.
    I'm sure he got his own two cents
    To share, if you'll jes lend an ear.
    He's real sincere.

Sit awhile and let me tell ya
What I've seen across the ages:
Guv'ments takin' people's money,
Takin' power out their wages.
It's outrageous.

I'm jes sayin' what I been seein'.
Ain't my fault – it's jes my role:
Robin-Hood the hardest workers
And pay out on the welfare dole.
That's the goal.

Leaders love me, claim to cut me,
But thanks to me their pockets bulge.
They'd rather give a man a free fish
With my taxes than a nudge.
You be the judge.

Cain't rely on life or freedom
Or the pursuit of happiness
Or fairness, justice, love, or wealth
"Nothin's sure 'cept Death 'n' Taxes"
'Round these parts, that is.

Tragically Distant

It's Thanksgiving again.
So happy to be off work,
When gatherings at a feast
Bring distant ones together…
But this year just feels wrong.
One doesn't have the time,
The other just bought a house
So money is tight this year –
And some just don't want to.
One lives down in Florida,
The other over in Texas,
Another up in Utah,
And more in California.
We're rather socially distant!
Our time, money, and interest
Don't come together often,
This year is no exception.
Maybe this sad feeling
Of being so tragically far
From those we love the most
Is what Thanksgiving's about.

Friends?

He didn't give you your half?
You told him three times and
Three times he said no?
You're mad and don't want to play
With him anymore. It's not fair.

She told on you when she did it too?
You didn't say anything though?
She always tattle-tells and
Cries to someone, blaming you.

He tells the teacher, and wants
You and your buddies to get in trouble?
Somehow they've been taught
To lie and deny, and you're right:
Who needs friends like these?

Observations

From the back of the room she
    Observes me, checks off the boxes on
        The rigid rubric, looks at my Plan,
            Execution and Delivery, and sizes
                Me down to a number on a rubric.
                From where I stand, it's obvious
            She will never notice my lost sleep,
        My conscious concern for my kids,
      How I think about my lessons as bigger
Than the myopic scale on her chart.

Can she understand my aims
Or possibly see the time spent perfecting my
Art? She doesn't see what I'm doing as art.
These visits are aimed at checking the
Bigger box of Professional Improvement
As a make-up mirror highlights
All the deep lines and blemishes.
If only she could know how proud I
Am of these: Evidence I did
More than just look with my eyes.

Those Clouds – What Teasers

These clouds –
See how they laugh at me
        with their friends.
Look how they turn to
                each other to mock me
                and my tiny ant-like
                powerlessness –
Dangling their legs atop
                their dormant Nevisian master,
                now emerald velvet,
They're acting the coveted
                part of the steamy plume,
"But you're just common run-o'-the-mill clouds!
You don't scare me,"
                I retort in my crescendoing
                concern.
The fear is sleeping for now.

The beach lady draping
                my lounge with towels
Tempers my anxiety:
"What can we do? Just pray,"
With a smile, like she won't
                stand for bullies.
"It's nature."
Sand like cinders;
All these lands are dark,
                ashy, earthy, raw, fire-birthed.

It could awake from its coma
        momentarily,
And I would be chased off
        this island paradise,
Fleeing, desperate for some
        other nearby speck
        in the ocean.

Those clouds –
Let them laugh and
        tease me.
I'll keep turning my
        beach chair around
To face that verdant, steep
        Goliath who lazily sleeps on,
        perhaps for ten more centuries.

They veil the mysterious
        humpbacked pinnacle,
Those clouds
        what teasers.
They tag the summit and
        swiftly run past.
They play their games and
        giggle,
For they know a secret they
        won't tell.

The Drips

Two pointy brown needles overhang the roof
 Dripping down their sharp fingernails the residue
  Of rain that came and left hours ago. The drops take
   Two whole seconds to grow at the tips, then three, as
   Less and less life-giving liquid flows.
    "More time, just a little more. Please!"
     Then it's four seconds in-between the
      Letting-go moments, of release.
       No more rain is coming, and the
        Watching is painfully slow, bitter,
         Hopeless, gut-punch sad.

          Now six seconds mark the parting
           Pieces, and the more time drains
            The more the sweet essence breaks
             Free. There is so much more to say,
              To do together, if there were time,
               But it's eight seconds, then ten. The
                Tears are shedding slower, drying up.
                 The hemorrhage is finishing, and it's
                  Easy to look away, but
                   Now is not the time.

                    The precious sanc
                     tity of Being i
                      s still present,
                       even once
                        the dri
                         ps st
                          op.

To Now

Click the switch on the lighter's handle
To light the wick of the Christmas candle
Sit back, breathe out, and just relax
So long as the glass has wax.

Keep up December's decorations
Past the New Year's celebrations
Savor the evergreen's scent; stall
Until all her needles fall.

Leave on the lights and ornaments
Send out presents with sentiments
Write every card, no matter how late
There is no time to wait.

Bake the cookies you "shouldn't" eat
Give away gifts to all you meet
So what if you drink too much? Anyhow,
Cheers to the moment: To now.

Brown Blanket

The gray tabby sniffs at the fuzzy brown blanket,
  Folded and familiar, laid in the morning sun.
The other two spent their final days and hours
  Bundled in this now-sacred shroud.

Maybe a scent still lingers – a distant memory, the fur
  Caught somewhere deep in the fibers there.
Maybe she knows its solemn power to soothe
  The bodily pangs of failing organs and old bones.

The silky comfort in the warm ray is all she asks,
  Lying long, paws overlaid, while the coffee brews.
O how the time is closing, with long naps and lazy looks,
  When she'll be swaddled in its brown embrace.

There are Things

There are things you'll
need to know that
I must show you:

How to love your
child more than your
self, how to spare

Your spouse the pain,
how to just wait,
and how to lose.

To win the fight
is but to lose
the war of love.

And to be first
can not be the
best, and the one

Who finds joy is
he who can put
his rights on hold.

These are things I
can say but acts
will be the proof.

Holy Ground

It has been asked where
I go to church, and I have lied.
It has been suggested that
I raise my son in these chambers
Where I was raised, but I do not.

It has been noted how often
I am busy, or traveling, or too tired
(Or too anything) to dress up in
The proper uniform for Sunday
Ceremonies. I just cannot.

It has been pointed out what
"The Church" really is, and yet the
Quotes come cascading down on me
From this book, that chapter and verse,
Again, again, like I forgot.

Is it for the music or prayer?
I can make my own here on this
Cliffside with the wind and waves
Crashing in my echoing ears.
Is it for that? No, I guess not.

Is it to gather in the same place
Once a week to remind ourselves how
We need each other to be complete
In this lonely world? Well,
What if I know a better spot?

This seaside promontory overlooking
The vastness of the oceans schools
Me on my antish smallness and
Delicate triviality where no stained glass,
Organ, pulpit, or priest has taught.

And it's been plainly said how
Children must be brought up in
These ways to follow the right path.
Is church the only holy ground
To learn God's beauty? Surely not.

Time is all we havE

Time is all we havE
It's what we most craV
Men waste this erA
'Ere realizing. LaugH

I have what you havE
Sunrises with deW

A new chance to feeL
Love, a place to strolL
Like in AustraliA

With money like thiS
Every moment I

Have cries out to bE
Allocated. I'M
Venturing this: I
Envy lives full spenT

There Are Stars

Some will say
seize the day
come what may
face the fray
run this race
don't be swayed.
Act the play
as the curtain closes.

    They may find
    peace of mind
    from the grind
    more defined
    when behind
    the long line.
    Just unwind
    as the day discloses.

        How to parse
        what we are!
        Time is sparse
        we reach far
        and work hard.
        Oh, take heart
        There are stars
        right under our noses.

B is for Butterflies

We fit. We yin and yang. It works.
One is always in the driver's seat, one wears the pants
is in the spotlight, on the stage.
There's always the one
who can talk to complete strangers, make
friends in the elevator, meet up with new people met online, or
strike up some chit-chat at the bar, high-five fellow dancers
at the concert and get numbers in the parking lot.

It's beautiful to watch, really,
since not all of us are programmed to
social-butterfly our way through life.
We read on the plane, drive through the parking lot,
write notes at the bar, and dance in our own quiet corner.
We are butterflies too,
but they won't notice us.
We don't rock the boat or make waves,
we're not the squeaky wheel,
and we prefer it that way.
Most days.

Then comes the time when we snap.
We make some noise for once and step on stage,
speak up and cry out for
a short moment of attention.
It's so uncalled for, it's downright aggressive
coming from the likes of us.
What's come over us?

They'll call us passive, but inwardly we are
quite actively dominant:
Type B personalities with little to say
since we just don't say it out loud.
They've named us introverted, reclusive…reserved
like we're not already sitting at the table,
like the lights are not on and nobody's home.
We're in there, damn it!
Planning and trying for somewhat different aims,
or maybe even the same ones –
how would *you* know?

They assume we're not getting anything done.
But we are the constant,
the pulse,
the bass rhythm,
the wind in your sails,
a deep presence.

Maybe the highs aren't so high, but
the lows aren't so low;
we're just the deadline,
the worker bees
with no flashy glamor.
We stand quietly by while you talk to
everyone else *but* us.
You will never fully see or hear us,
but damn it,
We're right here.

Last Confession

It's been…gosh, how many days since
My last confession? A lot.

Father, forgive me for I have sinned and I hear
You dole out absolution. I need some of that.

It all started when my type-A husband envisioned a
Road trip to 6 different cities in 6 days,
So yeah, I took a hotel pillow
For the car ride. Not my best moment.

My fog-brain went into a frenzy
And cleared out the soaps, shampoos
And in-room Keurig pods.
Maybe even a Kleenex box.

Then the Temptor presented me with the
Breakfast buffet. I came away
Loaded with caffeine and a purse full
Of tea bags, oatmeal packets,
And oranges "for the road". In my hyper state,
I must've grabbed enough hot cocoa mixes
And to-go cereals to attract attention, my conscience
Guilty only because of some unfriendly looks.

Otherwise, I don't even notice when my
Hands start scooping up nightstand pads
and pens, and other "included" items.
Is it true it'd be better to cut off my hands
Than to let them do this?
Well, I blame them for the many airline earbuds
I have somehow collected.
We should be punished I guess.

I figure my net worth is inching
Out of the red with every vanity set of
Q-tips and golf tees I'm offered.
It's just math.
But some may argue I'm stealing, so
I've come to check with you.
Is it really so wrong to take the extra
Toilet paper home?
Am I not entitled to handfuls of
Mints after dinner?

But is it True?

1. Like an elderly school teacher to a naughty young child, the moon gives me that look: Just a speck of dust in the breeze, just another aimless generation of walking noise. And the echoing fears of the cemeteries again ask, "But is it true?"
2. The seeds of faith went deep, almost strangling, so that on a random pew in whatever city, it's still the aching question of my middle-aged prime: "To believe is good, but is it true?" and the pulpits never seem to hear this sincere hymn.
3. The candle flickering away had a beginning and now slowly crawls back into bed at its latest hour. Why is it so wrong to doubt the eternal when nothing in this life shares even a shadow of that trait? Then again, what if it is true?
4. A shriveled witch must have locked herself down in the cell of my confused soul so that now when I hear that dear, sick Fill-in-the-Blank has "gone to be with the Lord" or "been called home", I wince and wonder,   "Did she?"
5. The delicious pleasure of the rare wine is that there are only so many drops and then the bottle is useless. Where would be the value of it if it just flowed from an everlasting faucet? I can't help feeling there must be a limit.
6. If we pray for life or healing and receive it, we praise God for his mercy. But more often we find that death comes and we accept that God knows best. Is he still merciful or are we too afraid to wonder if he's even there.
7. Some will quote the blessed scripture, that foundational bedrock, but even that was laid by a multitude of hopeful men who looked up at this same moon with optimism. Do their souls look down on my curiosity with disgust?

8. A simple mid-life crisis would be easier, a much more
    pleasurable distraction from the mundane reality that my
    accomplishments are nil and death is scratching his way
    into my disloyal limbs. The hourglass sands are going…

9. Blasphemy! some will claim when I wonder aloud whether
    the martyrs died for no great heavenly reward. They will
    not consider that centuries of religious history, all devout
    and sincere, may be the wishful thinking inside all of us.

10. But is it *true*? Can I trust in an endless afterlife? No claims
    of certainty can convince me. But it is that gripping effort
    of grasping for the hope of more life after all is lost in this
    realm that makes me reconsider. Hope itself is life-giving.

Ten Days of Christmas on the Road

In the ten days on either side of
Christmas and New Year's, we drove a
Ziggy-zagged swath of Texas to Florida,
North Carolina to Mississippi, then home.
And on every side, every day, as I'm
Doing the lion's share of the steering, the
Cross-country miles are marked by at least
A hundred bodies. Dead, beside the
ROAD.

I see why: with speed limits of 75, which
Means I can get away with 83, there is no slowing
Down on a dime if (when!) they wander into the
Lane. I didn't hit any of these dearly departed
Deer with their tongues lolling out, but I
Could have. A few coyotes with their salt-n-pepper
Coats were curled as if sleeping, stopped
just as they might have been on the scent of a
KILL.

Years ago, I hit a squirrel that darted out
Of the woods, quicker than I could react.
Though the remorse was deep, nothing could
Retract what had been done. Now I spy other poor
Little things: armadillos still munching on grass
Not two feet from all these whizzing wheels,
Free-range dogs romping carelessly yards away.
Oh, I sure hope they don't get hit like these
HAD.

As miles turn into hours and nights, I watch
With extra caution to prevent another case of
Bloated bellies, contorted bodies, some just fur
After months, maybe years, of decay. Forgotten.
With barely a chance to get a good look, there is
A steadily seeping numbness — deadness of feeling —
So grossly they are mangled; but they beg
To be seen, that I should notice and treasure
LIFE.

Love in Code

Right about the time you stop worrying that your little one will
fall down stairs or electrocute a finger, they begin riding bikes to a
friend's and stay home while you're out at a late concert.
They make the golf team, and you stop worrying.

Right about that time, you realize that although he will need you
less and less, and of course you will worry even when it's
pointless, you keep on helicoptering around just in case there's the
slightest possibility that you'll be needed.

"Don't forget a belt…Did you remember your lunch?…Text me
when you get there."
(I   love   you)

Right around this time, you remember that your own aging parents
have versions of these same phrases. Each passing year reminds
them to give their love more and perhaps be forgotten less easily,
and so they repeat them like an old church chorus:

"Drive carefully…I'm cooking your favorite dinner…Let me
check your oil before you leave."
(I   love   you)

It's right about this time you actually get it, what it is they're trying
to say. As you sit alone on a hotel balcony with a trembling coffee
cup and a view of the mountains, you tear up and sob through the
memories of the phrases they always used to say.

"I'll be praying…It's O.K. honey – we all make mistakes…Thanks
for calling."

Our Esperanza

Hace un año que la familia yo he visto.
And someone always grabs my son and says
"Tu hijo es más alto y más guapo"
To them his changes make him marvelous.

Y mientras su crecimiento discuten
I see these loved ones have aged
And they go on fawning and admiring, unfazed
Y nuestras historias y noticias disfrutan.

With all our optimism, it's youth we praise
Pero cada década tiene valor
With each New Year we hope for better days
Con más momentos de amor.

When young we're propelled by our hopes
Y por nuestras memorias cuando viejos.

POP

I'd like to think it takes a lot to send me into a
spiraling rage but I guess it takes
no time at all.
This basketball season has been a test of my character.

He showed his the day the tryouts list came out: "I know I should
be embarrassed to be the only 8th grader on the B team,
but I'm not. Those other guys are way better than me and this way
I'll get more playing time."

Modest. True?
I couldn't tell,
but since it didn't seem to bother him
I went with it.

   For two whole months he started the game
   with the jump ball, really got better, played
   most of each game, helped the team go from
   losing streaks to sometimes winning, and –
   here's the best part –
   developed self-confidence…
   That apparently can POP like a water balloon.

So my friend says over coffee mid-season, "The A team coaches
will probably invite him to the district tournament at the end of the
season since he's an 8th grader. That's what they did last year" and
how my pride swelled when he was!

He and 4 other players.

Maybe it was the growing despair on the 5 benched guys that
made my blood boil with each passing quarter. Or the
fact that these other teams had way more players
yet still found a way to sub them in.

Finally, at the thought of going to Thursday night's last two games
that would decide the district winner, I said, "Well, what's the
argument *for* going, even if you sit on the bench?"
"My friends and Coach will be 1% happier but I still won't play."

So we didn't go.
The damage was already done.

POP

Intentional

I look into the small wooden box with Mackey's ashes and wonder,
"Where did he go, Cat Heaven?" No, no of course not,
as much as I wish I were wrong.
So then why would there be a Human Heaven if we
so easily dismiss one for animals?
Maybe Heaven just isn't there.

Then I go to a funeral or learn that someone is terminally ill
and again I run face-on into the idea of life after death.
What's a funeral service without this assumption?
It's the only idea that lessens the pain of severe loss and grief.
(And I wouldn't know. No one I've been close to has died yet.
When they do, though, how badly will I need Heaven to be real?)

Last week I read a book by Stephen Hawking delicately addressing
the idea that, well, science doesn't support the presence of God,
and in fact it actually supports other realities. So again the rug of
my upbringing is shifted further out from under me. What if God
isn't the one who created the universe and there is no spiritual
afterlife? These seem like fair questions.

It would mean that the Bible is written by well-meaning men and
should not be the centerpiece of one's life. Maybe it carries
wisdom and general truths but perhaps not the only source.
It would make church attendance more of a ritual with the real
value being community. All other religions, for that matter,
would equally be tempered.

Still, we send our son to a Christian school where chapel services
three times a week give him the Biblical foundation we've had,
with all the fabric of faith. It wasn't enough though, when we
began asking harder questions. What happens when we die?
Why are we so grievously destroyed by loss? Could it be that we
know somewhere deep down that it means an end?

At funerals, the religious person speaks of seeing the person again
and being together for eternity. Even in the movies, bodies are
returned to the prime of their lives. Is it just too raw to say that
they're gone and they lived their life well, and we will miss them,
and never be the same, and try to remember all they taught us, and
(since life is so short) live in a more intentional way?

Painting This Night's Canvas

On a cloudless night past late,
with the moonlight painting ghostly-whitish squares on the floor
where the table used to be,
there is a restless agitation in the black air and
those who normally sleep soundly are wide awake with worry.
The wars have come into our own land and youth choose
angry sides and there is no safe side to choose. Both sides justify.
These three days remaining
before the big move further west leaves static in the chest:
this limbo week is a no-man's wasteland
and the goodbyes will be permanently sealed.
The close of one year and the unknown of the summer months, the
page is now turning
that brings the promise of more happiness,
at the cost of everything familiar,
and having moved many times before, the promise isn't trusted.
So there is naturally a shadowy fear painting this night's canvas
with only a few stars and a half-hearted moon.
The family I long to see will come for a fleeting visit and the
whole time we will both
show our love in strange and incoherent languages,
missing the messages like a voicemail
to a wrong number.

Spotter

They must learn how to fall asleep on their
own so lay them down in their crib awake.

Now he wants to go to the weight room and asks me to spot him.
"Don't grab the bar until I absolutely can't do it on my own"
he instructs as I look down over the bench press, skeptical.

Then his first girlfriend breaks up with him a month
after he moves away, and he knows it's coming.
I get up from bed once the house is sleeping to
read what his girlfriend wrote to break up.
It must've hurt to hear such things.
I'm the spotter. What do I do?

Let struggle be the teacher.
Be there, just in case.

Turn Right

Why do the minor frills distract and distort
our contentment so?
How they can dress up a pig,
but it's just for show.
Only a very few things matter when you
fall to sleep at night:
The people – only the people – and
making wrongs turn right.

Not a Run-on

The gift
is a hand-stitched pickle propped up on a stand holding a sign that
says, "You're a Big Dill" accompanied by a Visa card, a fairy
necklace that my nieces picked out, a Tennessee candle that smells
of vanilla and whisky, and a fancy dinner of chicken piccata – oh,
and red wine! – along with all the colorful envelopes in the mail
packed with bulging birthday wishes (making a trip to the mailbox
feel like a journey back to childhood), as well as the mini bundt
cakes the neighbors brought over; however, the real gift
is being 45…
and still finding love.

www.ingramcontent.com/pod-product-compliance
Lightning Source LLC
Chambersburg PA
CBHW072141150726
48002CB00004B/1567